CREATURES IN WHITE

POLAR BEARS

For Tim,
who loves nature and books, especially
polar bears and polar bear books.

W. P.

Published by Silver Press
A Division of Simon & Schuster
299 Jefferson Road, Parsippany, NJ 07054

Designed by Brooks Design

Printed in the United States of America

ISBN 0-382-39327-9 (LSB) 10 9 8 7 6 5 4 3 2
ISBN 0-382-39326-0 (PBK) 10 9 8 7 6 5 4 3 2

Library of Congress Cataloging-in-Publication Data
Pfeffer, Wendy.
Polar bears/by Wendy Pfeffer.
p. cm.–(Creatures in white)
Summary: The life cycle and physical characteristics of the polar bear.
1. Polar bear–Juvenile literature. [1. Polar bear. 2. Bears.] I. Title. II. Series: Pfeffer, Wendy. Creatures in White.
QL737.C27P46 1997 95-25790
599.74'446–dc20 CIP AC

Photo credits: Photo research by Susan Van Etten; Cover, Bryn Campbell/©Tony Stone Worldwide; 2-3, ©Wayne Lynch/DRK Photo; 4-5, ©Thomas D. Mangelsen/Peter Arnold, Inc.; 6-7, ©B. & C. Alexander; 8-9, ©Thomas D. Mangelsen/Peter Arnold, Inc.; 10-11, ©Mittet Foto/Tony Stone Worldwide; 12-13, ©Wayne Lynch/DRK Photo; 14-15, ©Gary Schultz/Alaska Stock Images; 16-17, ©Daryl Pederson/Alaska Stock Images; 18-19, ©B. & C. Alexander; 20-21, ©S.J. Krasemann/Peter Arnold, Inc.; 22-23, ©Masterfile; 24-25, ©David C. Fritts/Animals, Animals; 26-27,©Mike Macri/ Masterfile; 28-29, ©Mike Macri/ Masterfile; 30, ©Gerard Lacz/Animals, Animals; 30, ©B. & C. Alexander; 31, ©B. & C. Alexander; 31, ©1994, Steve Kaufman/Peter Arnold, Inc.; 31, ©Wayne Lynch/Masterfile; End Paper, ©Thomas D. Mangelsen/Peter Arnold, Inc.; Back Cover, ©B. & C. Alexander.

Silver Press
Parsippany, New Jersey

Near the North Pole, surrounded by ice and snow, polar bears live in a frozen world. In polar bear country, even the ocean freezes.

Polar bears survive the cold because they have two fur coats: one of long white fur over one of short white fur. Both coats cover a layer of skin and four inches of fat. Polar bears' coats are warmer than any coat you wear—and bigger, too.

A large male polar bear stands over nine feet tall and weighs about 1,000 pounds (450 kg). Where is that huge polar bear? He's camouflaged. His white coat blends in with the white snow and hides him from sight. The female polar bear with him is camouflaged, too.

Later, as the male bear ambles over ice floes, the female bear wanders inland to prepare for winter. In a deep snowdrift the she-bear uses her sharp claws as shovels to hollow out a long, narrow tunnel. She digs for days.

At the end of the tunnel, she carves out a cave, which becomes her winter den. Drifting snow covers up the entrance. In the winter the Arctic stays dark all day and all night.

An arctic fox passes the den searching for food it stored in the fall. A fat, hairy reindeer also wanders by, finding tasty clumps of grass under the snow.

The male polar bear does not hibernate. He lumbers past, hunting for food. He may catch a musk ox to eat. If not, he'll use his own fat for energy or return to the ocean to hunt seals. Where is the she-bear?

She's cozy in her den, protected from the cold under a thick blanket of freshly fallen snow. She's alone, but not for long.

By midwinter the she-bear, that weighs about 700 pounds, gives birth to two cubs. Each cub weighs about one pound—less than you weighed when you were born!

Her helpless, toothless babies are the size of little guinea pigs. She licks her babies. They start to breathe.

She snuggles them close. They can't see her yet, but they can feel her warmth. Nestled in her snowy white fur, they nurse on their mother's creamy, rich milk. Her body makes milk even though she doesn't eat all winter. The snow den is peaceful for the tired mother bear and her sleepy cubs.

But not for long. In a few weeks, the cubs' eyes open. For the rest of the winter, the roly-poly cubs chase each other, wrestle up and down the tunnel, and climb all over their weary mother.

By spring each cub is about the size of a small dog and has grown thick white fur, sharp claws, and teeth. After the long winter the mother bear is hungry. She crawls through the tunnel, scoops out some snow, and looks outside.

The cubs follow their mother and see a new world . . . a world of white, bright with sunlight, not like their dark den. The cubs feel their new world . . . cold, not like their warm den. They hear their new world . . . quiet, just like their winter den.

The cubs are not ready to survive in this new world. Their visits outside the den must be short. The cubs run, romp, hide, climb up and slide down snowdrifts, building muscles, and getting strong–while the mother bear relaxes in the sun.

Soon they're ready to follow her to the ocean to find food. During the journey the mother bear tries to catch a reindeer, but it's too fast for her. So are the birds that have returned from the south.

The cubs thrive on mother's milk, so they have no need to eat birds or reindeer meat. They jump and play along the way.

The mother bear and her cubs finally reach the ocean. They wander across huge chunks of floating ice. Thick pads of fur on the bottom of the bears' feet shield their paws from the cold and keep the bears from slipping on the ice.

Suddenly the mother bear senses danger! A walrus with long, pointed tusks rests on the ice. The mother bear leads her cubs safely in a wide circle around the drowsy but dangerous animal.

Further along, sleeping in the sun, lies a ringed seal, the mother bear's favorite food. The fluffy white cubs sit still, camouflaged on the snow, and watch their mother.

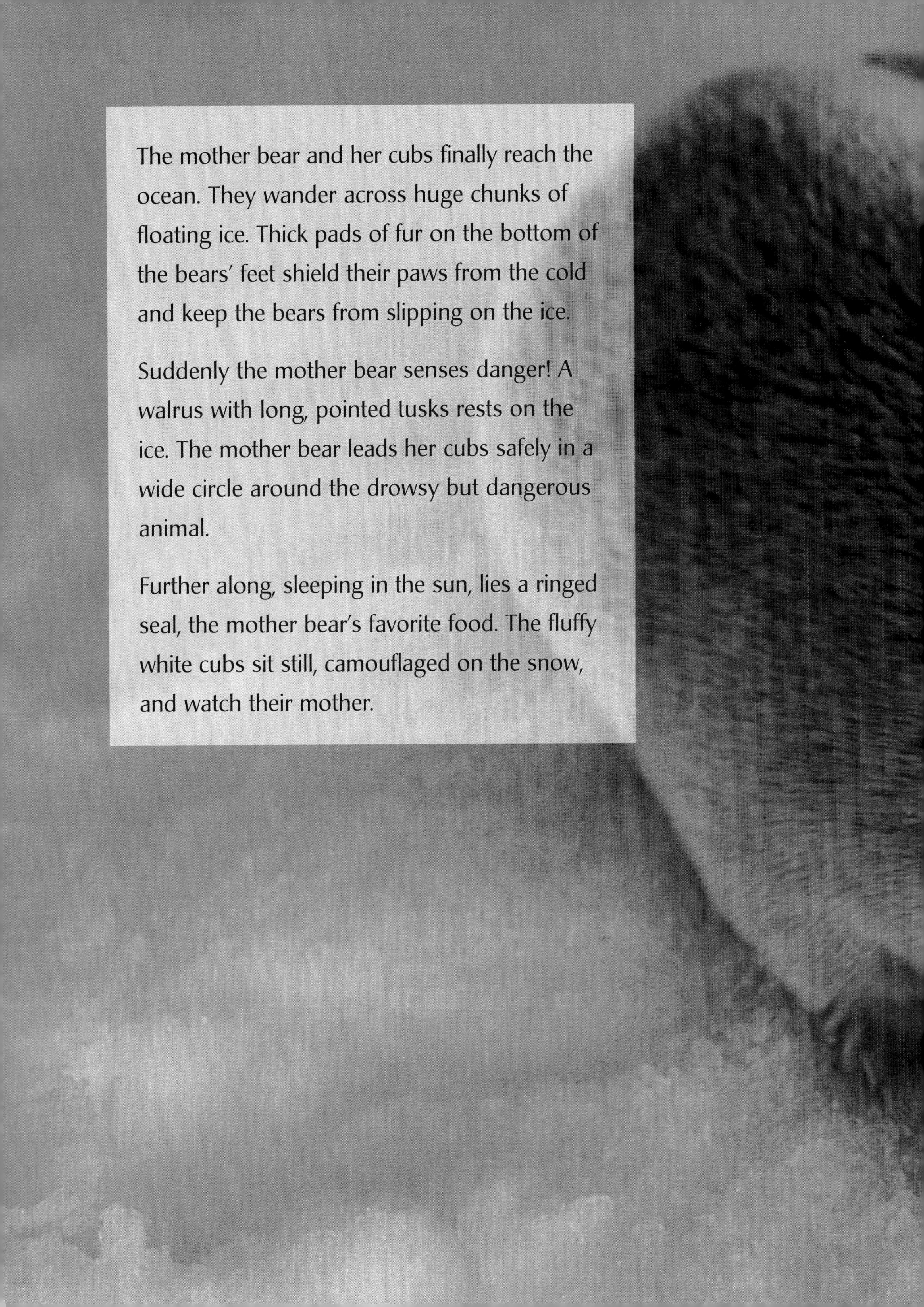

Sometimes the big white bear covers her dark nose with one paw. This keeps her camouflaged as she sneaks over the ice toward the seal.

Quietly she lies down. Slowly she crawls forward. Carefully she moves nearer. Quickly she pounces on the seal, then lumbers back to her cubs.

The cubs get their first taste of seal, but still need mother's milk to grow. The mother bear eats only the skin and fat of her prey. She leaves the meat which is eaten by other animals who wander by.

Mother and her cubs continue to roam over the sea ice which drifts with the wind and the flow of the water. Suddenly the cubs belly-flop into the ocean.

The mother bear flops into the icy water, too. The thick fur coats that keep the bears warm in winter act like raincoats, shedding water when they swim. The bears paddle with their front feet, steer with their hind feet, and stop once in a while to eat seaweed. The bears spend many spring days like this in the water.

Slowly the days get longer and warmer. Summer arrives with a supply of berries and grasses for the bears to eat. The white snow melts, and the brown earth appears. Snowy white fur doesn't camouflage polar bears in summer.

If the cubs get too hot in their fur coats, the mother bear shows them how to dig into the ground, where the soil is still frozen. Then the cubs sit and let the chilled earth cool their bodies.

In the fall the mother bear teaches the cubs to use their big paws to scoop tasty fish out of swift flowing streams.

When winter comes again, the mother bear does not dig a den. Her cubs must learn about the cold dark world of winter.

The three hunt for food, then curl up and sleep, facing away from the wind. They may dig a shallow shelter if a blizzard blows. When the storm is over, their search for food continues. In just one year, the cubs have grown from the size of a guinea pig to the size of a man.

In one more year the cubs are almost as big as their mother. Now, two years old, they defend themselves, swim, hunt, and catch their own food.

When spring comes, something inside the young bears tells them, "Wander away. Go on your own." The mother bear is ready to start another family, so she gives them a nudge.

They wander away . . . lumbering over ice floes and white snow, camouflaged from danger and able to survive in a frozen world.

Bear Facts

- The polar bear is the only bear in the world that looks all white.
- A polar bear is the world's largest land-living carnivorous animal.
- The temperature inside a mother polar bear's den might be 40 degrees warmer than the temperature outside.
- Polar bears sometimes slide down slippery slopes on their bellies, with their legs stretched out.
- No other four-footed mammal can swim as fast as a polar bear.
- Polar bears can swim far, too—50 miles (80km) without stopping.

- A fully grown polar bear's greatest enemy is the killer whale.

- Polar bears have an excellent sense of smell. They can smell a dead whale that is 20 miles away.

- Polar bears are not sociable creatures. One polar bear will pass another, leaving the length of a soccer field between them.

- Polar bears do not hibernate. Only mother bears with babies stay in a den all winter.

- A polar bear's front feet are somewhat webbed. They make great swimming flippers.

- A polar bear's feet are extra wide. They act as snowshoes to keep the bear on top of the snow.

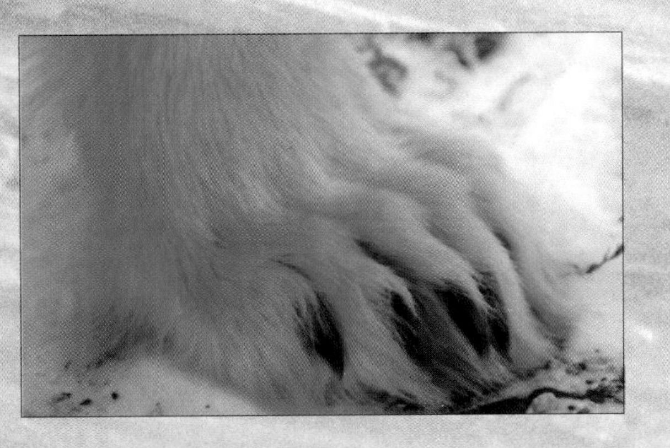

WHERE IN THE WORLD ARE POLAR BEARS?

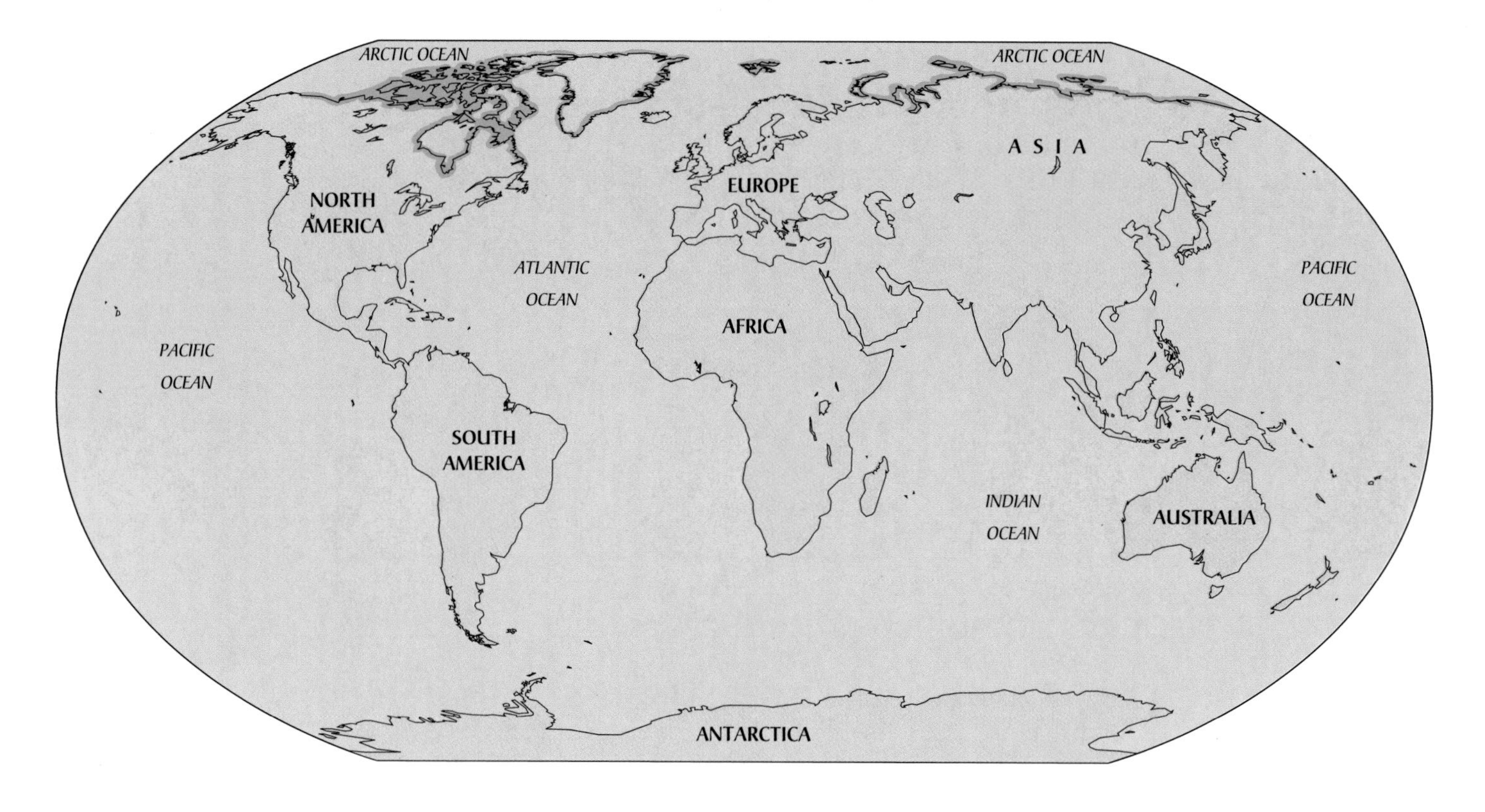

Polar bears live here